GrowForth Kids Co.

SMART CHOICES

The Economics of Everyday Decisions

I0560792

Matthew MacMillan
and Scott MacMillan

GROW FORTH

PRESS
—BY GRAMMAR FACTORY—

Grow Forth Kids
MacMillan Company Limited
25 Telegram Mews, 39th Floor, Suite 3906
Toronto, Ontario, Canada
M5V 3Z1

www.growforthpress.com

MacMillan, Matthew and Scott MacMillan
GrowForth Kids Co: Smart Choices: The Economics of Everyday Decisions /
Matthew MacMillan and Scott MacMillan.

Paperback ISBN 978-1-998528-55-4
Hardcover ISBN 978-1-998528-57-8
eBook ISBN 978-1-998528-56-1

1. JNF013050 JUVENILE NONFICTION / Business & Economics / General.
2. JNF013030 JUVENILE NONFICTION / Business & Economics / Personal Finance.
3. JNF000000 JUVENILE NONFICTION / General.

Production Credits
Book production and editorial services by Grammar Factory (www.grammarfactory.com)

Disclaimer
The material in this publication is of the nature of general comment only and does not represent professional advice. It is not intended to provide specific guidance for particular circumstances, and it should not be relied on as the basis for any decision to take action or not take action on any matter which it covers. Readers should obtain professional advice where appropriate, before making any such decision. To the maximum extent permitted by law, the author and publisher disclaim all responsibility and liability to any person, arising directly or indirectly from any person taking or not taking action based on the information in this publication.

Contents

PART 4: BIG-PICTURE DECISION-MAKING
Seeing beyond yourself

Business Brain Challenge
Can You Plan a Smart Choice?   51

BACK POCKET BONUSES

Introduction

Welcome to GrowForth Kids Co.

Hi – we're so glad you're here again!

Welcome back to **GrowForth Kids Co.** – where curious kids like you learn how the world really works. Not just in school or textbooks, but in real life... with real choices, real challenges, and real ways to build something awesome.

"What's left to learn after money?"

Well, money's just the start! What really shapes your life is how you make decisions.

You're already making choices every day – like how to spend your time, what to save your money for, which hobbies to try, or even how to balance fun and schoolwork. Every one of those choices comes with a tradeoff, a cost, and an opportunity.

This book is your next-level toolkit.

Inside, you'll learn:

- How to spot hidden costs and tradeoffs in everyday decisions
- How to think smart when small choices add up
- How to weigh risks, rewards, and priorities
- And how to understand why doing the right thing often matters more than doing the easy thing.

Each chapter breaks down one important idea – in plain, kid-friendly language – with relatable examples and a sketch to help you picture it. At the end of each one, there's a "Try This!" section with a small challenge you can try on your own or with a grown-up.

And when you finish the book?

You'll take on a **GrowForth Kids Co. Business Brain Challenge** to put your smart decision-making skills into action. (It's fun. Promise.)

Let's get going. Your decision-making brain is ready to grow forth. 🌱

Part 1

Why Every Choice Matters

How little decisions shape big outcomes

"Life is a matter of choices, and every choice you make makes you."

— John C. Maxwell, leadership expert

Every day, you make hundreds of choices. Big ones, like what to do with your weekend, and small ones, like which snack to grab or what to watch next.

But here's the surprise: Even tiny choices **add up** – and they shape the kind of person you become.

In this section, you'll learn:

- Why choosing one thing means giving up something else *(opportunity cost)*
- How to avoid getting stuck on past decisions *(sunk cost)*
- How to think smart when you can't have everything *(tradeoffs)*
- Why knowing the difference between *needs and wants* matters (quick recap)
- What your time is really worth *(effective hourly rate)*

Great decision-making isn't about being perfect. It's about learning to spot what matters – and practicing how to choose wisely.

Ready? Let's dive in.

1

Opportunity Cost

What you give up when you choose something else

What it means

Every time you make a choice, you're also **giving up** the next-best thing you could have done instead.

That "missed" thing is called your **opportunity cost**.

It's not just about money – it's also about time, effort, and attention. Smart thinkers always ask: *What am I giving up by picking this?*

Here's an example

Let's say you have one free hour after school.

You could:

- Play video games
- Go for a bike ride
- Work on a craft project

You pick video games.

Your **opportunity cost** is whatever fun or value you missed by not choosing the other two.

It's not always about making the "perfect" choice – it's about knowing that choosing one thing means skipping something else.

Why it's important

Understanding opportunity cost helps you:

- Think carefully about your choices
- Avoid wasting time or money on things that don't matter
- Focus on what brings you the most value or happiness
- Learn to plan ahead

Every choice has a hidden cost – even if you don't see it right away.

Try this!

Make a list of three things you could do this afternoon.

Now pick one.

Ask yourself: *What did I give up by choosing this?*

Would you make the same choice again tomorrow?

2

Sunk Cost

Why past actions shouldn't trap future decisions

What it means

A **sunk cost** is money, time, or effort you've already spent – and you can't get it back.

The tricky part? We often let sunk costs push us to keep going, even when we should stop.

But smart thinkers know:
past costs shouldn't control future choices.

Here's an example

Imagine you spend $10 on a movie ticket.

Halfway through, you realize you're not enjoying the movie. You think, *"I paid for this, so I should stay."*

But here's the truth:

The $10 is **already gone** (sunk cost).

You should decide based on what's best now – do you *want* to stay, or would you be happier doing something else?

Why it's important

Understanding sunk costs helps you:

- Stop wasting time or money on things that aren't working
- Make smarter, more forward-looking decisions
- Avoid throwing "good" effort after "bad"
- Focus on what's still possible, not what's already lost

It's okay to change your mind when things change.

Try this!

Think of something you've kept doing just because you already started – like a game, a book, or a hobby.

Would you keep going if you were starting fresh today?

If not, maybe it's time to let go!

3

Tradeoffs

You can't have everything, so choose wisely

What it means

A **tradeoff** is what you give up when you choose one thing over another.

It's a lot like opportunity cost – but it focuses more on the fact that **you can't have everything at once**. Life is full of limits: time, money, energy. That's why every choice requires tradeoffs.

Here's an example

Let's say you have $10 to spend at a fair.

You could:

- Buy a toy you've been eyeing
- Get snacks and drinks for yourself and a friend
- Play games at the prize booths

You can't do all three – not with just $10.

So you have to decide: *What matters most to me right now?*

That's the heart of tradeoffs.

Why it's important

Understanding tradeoffs helps you:

- Make intentional choices
- Plan ahead for what you really care about
- Feel more confident about saying "yes" or "no"
- Avoid regret by focusing on what matters most

Smart decision-makers weigh the tradeoffs before they act.

Try this!

Think of a time you had to choose between two or three good options.

What did you pick?

What did you give up?

If you could do it again, would you make the same tradeoff?

4

Needs vs. Wants
(Quick Recap)
Smart choices start with knowing the difference

What it means

We covered this in Book 1 (*How Money Works*), but it's so important we're giving it a quick recap here!

A **need** is something you must have to live – like food, water, clothes, or a place to sleep.

A **want** is something you like or enjoy but don't need to survive – like toys, video games, treats, or cool gadgets.

Both are okay! But knowing the difference helps you make smarter choices.

Here's an example

Let's say you're deciding what to spend your allowance on.

You need: A warm coat for winter

You want: A new video game or extra snacks

If you don't get the coat, you'll be cold.

If you skip the game, you might miss out on fun – but you'll still be okay.

Understanding needs vs. wants helps you prioritize.

Why it's important

Knowing the difference helps you:

- Make better spending choices
- Plan for important things first
- Avoid running out of money or resources for your needs
- Appreciate your wants without mixing them up with must-haves

Smart decision-makers cover their needs before chasing their wants.

Try this!

Make two lists:

1. Three things you need this month
2. Three things you want this month

Look at your time, money, or effort.

Are you giving your needs the attention they deserve?

5

Effective Hourly Rate
(EHR)

What your time is really worth

What it means

Your **Effective Hourly Rate (EHR)** is how much money you're really making for each hour you work.

It's not just about how much you *earn* – it's about how much you keep after subtracting your time, effort, and costs.

Knowing your EHR helps you know if something is worth your time.

Here's an example

Let's say you run a small dog-walking business. You earn $20 each weekend, but you spend:

- 4 hours walking dogs
- 1 hour traveling
- $5 on dog treats

So:

- Total time = 5 hours
- Total money = $20 – $5 = $15 profit

Your EHR = $15 ÷ 5 hours = **$3 per hour**.

Not bad! But knowing this lets you compare: Would babysitting, chores, or another project earn you more per hour?

Why it's important

Understanding your EHR helps you:

- See the true value of your time
- Compare different jobs, projects, or side hustles
- Focus on activities that give the most return
- Avoid wasting time on things that aren't worth the effort

Smart thinkers look beyond just "how much" – they ask, how much given the time spent.

Try this!

Think of something you did recently to earn money.

Write down:

1. How much money you made
2. How many total hours you spent
3. What you'd earn **per hour**

Is there a way to raise your EHR next time?

Part 2

Thinking at the Margins

How small changes
can make a big difference

"Small habits don't add up – they compound."
— James Clear, author of *Atomic Habits*

Big decisions get a lot of attention.

But here's a secret: **small decisions matter, too**.

In fact, learning to think carefully about tiny changes – like spending one more dollar, adding one more hour, or doing one more task – can help you unlock big benefits (or avoid big mistakes).

In this section, you'll learn:

- How to figure out the extra good you get from doing just a little more *(marginal benefit)*
- How to measure the extra cost of adding one more *(marginal cost)*
- Why doing more doesn't always mean getting more *(diminishing marginal returns)*
- How to focus on what matters most *(the 80/20 rule)*
- And why work often stretches to fill the time you give it *(Parkinson's Law)*

Smart decision-makers pay attention at the edges – where small choices create big results.

Ready? Let's sharpen those margin-thinking skills!

6

Marginal Benefit

The extra good you get from doing a little more

What it means

Marginal benefit is the extra benefit or satisfaction you get from adding **one more** of something.

It's not about the total – it's about the next step.

Smart thinkers always ask: *"If I do just a bit more, is it still worth it?"*

Here's an example

You're baking cookies.

- Adding 5 chocolate chips? Delicious.
- Adding 10 chocolate chips? Even better.
- Adding 50 chocolate chips? Hmm... now it's just a melted mess!

The marginal benefit is how much *extra* enjoyment you get from adding each chip – and at some point, the benefit stops being worth it.

Why it's important

Understanding marginal benefit helps you:

- Spot when adding more is worth it
- Recognize when you've hit the "sweet spot"
- Avoid wasting time, effort, or resources chasing tiny gains
- Focus on actions that bring the biggest payoff

It's not just about *doing more* – it's about doing what matters most.

Try this!

Pick a fun activity, like practicing a sport or drawing.

Spend 10 minutes doing it.

Ask yourself:

- If you did **10 more minutes**, would you enjoy it more or less?
- Is the extra time still worth it?

That's marginal benefit in action.

7

Marginal Cost

The extra cost
of doing a little more

What it means

Marginal cost is the extra cost (time, money, effort) you need to pay to add one more of something.

It's not about the total cost – it's about the cost of the next step.

Smart thinkers always ask: *"If I do just a bit more, what extra will it cost me?"*

Here's an example

You're running a lemonade stand.

- You've already made 10 cups.
- You want to make 1 more.

To do that, you'll need:

- More lemons and sugar = more money
- More time mixing and selling = more effort
- Maybe more cups = more supplies

The marginal cost is the cost of making that **11th cup** – not the cost of all the cups together.

Why it's important

Understanding marginal cost helps you:

- Compare whether the extra cost is worth the extra benefit
- Avoid spending more on something that isn't paying off
- Make smarter, more efficient choices
- Use your resources wisely

It's all about making sure the "next" step makes sense.

Try this!

Think of a task you're doing – like putting away toys or making bracelets. If you wanted to put away or make just **one more**, what would it cost you? Would the extra time or effort be worth it?

That's marginal cost at work.

8

Diminishing Marginal Returns

Why more isn't always better

What it means

Diminishing marginal returns means that at some point, adding more effort, resources, or *even fun stuff* gives you **less** extra benefit than before.

At first, every little bit helps – but after a while, doing or having *more* doesn't always mean *getting* more. Sometimes, it even makes things worse!

Here's an example

You're eating a big bowl of ice cream.

- The **first** bite? Amazing!
- The **fifth** bite? Still pretty good.
- The **tenth** bite? Hmm... not as exciting.
- The **fifteenth** bite? You're full – maybe even starting to feel sick!

The extra benefit (return) you get **shrinks** as you keep adding more.

This doesn't just apply to food – it also applies to studying, practicing, or spending money.

At some point, doing or having more stops adding value.

Why it's important

Recognizing diminishing marginal returns helps you:

- Avoid wasting time, effort, or resources on things that aren't helping
- Know when to stop or switch strategies
- Focus on what's really working
- Stay balanced and avoid burnout (or tummy aches!)

Smart thinkers don't just push harder – they push **smarter**.

Try this!

Think about something you've done recently – like playing a game, practicing a sport, or eating a treat.

Did you notice a point where the fun or benefit started to shrink?

That's your brain spotting diminishing marginal returns!

9

The 80/20 Rule
(Pareto Principle)

Focus on the few things that matter most

What it means

The **80/20 Rule** (known as the *Pareto Principle*) says that in many situations, **80% of the results come from just 20% of the effort or input.**

In other words, a small number of things often create the biggest impact.

Smart thinkers figure out *which* things matter most – and focus their time, energy, or money there.

Here's an example

You open your toy box.

- You own **20 toys**.
- You play with **4 favorites** over and over.
- The other 16? They sit on the shelf most of the time.

That's the 80/20 Rule in action:

80% of your fun comes from 20% of your toys!

Why it's important

Understanding the 80/20 Rule helps you:

- Focus on what really matters
- Avoid wasting time on things with tiny payoffs
- Make smart choices about where to put your energy or money
- Get bigger results with less effort

Smart thinkers work smarter, not just harder.

Try this!

Look at something you use often – maybe apps, games, clothes, or hobbies.

What are the **few** things you use or enjoy the most?

Are there things you're spending time or money on that don't add much value? Maybe you could sell or donate toys you don't use.

That's your chance to apply the 80/20 Rule!

10

Parkinson's Law

Why work stretches to fill the time you give it

What it means

Parkinson's Law is named after Cyril Northcote Parkinson, a British historian who studied how people work.

He noticed something funny:

A task will take **as long as the time you give it**.

If you set a long deadline, the work will expand and stretch to fill that time – even if it doesn't *really* need that long.

Smart thinkers set the right amount of time to stay focused and efficient.

Here's an example

You have a school project due in two weeks.

- If you give yourself the whole two weeks? You might waste time, procrastinate, or overcomplicate things.
- If you set a goal to finish it in three focused afternoons? You might get it done faster and with less stress.

The task grows or shrinks to match the time you allow.

Why it's important

Understanding Parkinson's Law helps you:

- Avoid wasting time by setting clear, short deadlines
- Stay focused and work efficiently
- Avoid "busy work" that doesn't improve the result
- Free up time for other fun or valuable things

Smart thinkers manage their time on purpose.

Try this!

Pick a small task, like tidying your room or finishing a worksheet.

Challenge yourself to **finish it faster** than usual – without rushing sloppily!

Notice how your focus improves when you limit the time.

Part 3

Negotiation and Smart Decisions

How to make good deals and stick to your goals

"In life, you don't get what you deserve, you get what you negotiate."

— Chester L. Karrass, negotiation expert

Making smart choices isn't just about thinking things through — sometimes, it's about **working with others**.

In this section, you'll learn:

- How to prepare a backup plan before making a deal *(BATNA)*
- How the first number can shape the whole conversation *(anchoring)*
- Why giving often leads to getting *(reciprocity)*
- How to start with your purpose in mind *(starting with why)*
- And how to focus on what matters most *(prioritization)*

Smart thinkers know that negotiation isn't about "winning" — it's about finding the best outcome, sticking to your goals, and creating value for everyone involved.

Let's get into it!

11

BATNA
(Best Alternative to a Negotiated Agreement)

Always have a backup plan

What it means

BATNA stands for **Best Alternative to a Negotiated Agreement.**

In simple terms, it means: *What's your backup plan if a deal doesn't work out?*

Smart negotiators figure out their BATNA before they start talking. That way, they know when to walk away and when to say yes.

Here's an example

You want to go to your friend's house after school to work on a song you're writing together.

Before you ask your parents, you think:

- What if they say no?
- Maybe my friend can come over to our house.
- Maybe we can schedule it for the weekend instead.
- Maybe we can work on it over a video call.

Which of these would you choose next? That's your **BATNA** – the best backup plan if your first idea doesn't work out.

Knowing your BATNA makes you **stronger** when you ask, because you have other options ready.

Why it's important

Understanding your BATNA helps you:

- Negotiate with confidence
- Avoid bad deals you'll regret later
- Know when to walk away
- Make better, smarter agreements

Smart thinkers always have a backup plan.

Try this!

Think of a trade or deal you might want to make — like swapping snacks, toys, or chores.

Before you ask, write down: *What's your best alternative if they say no?*

That's your BATNA in action!

12

Anchoring

First numbers shape final deals

What it means

Anchoring is when the **first number** or idea in a conversation pulls everything else closer to it.

In a negotiation, the first number someone says can act like an "anchor" – even if it's random or unfair. Smart negotiators understand how anchors work and use them carefully.

Here's an example

You're selling a used video game.

- Your friend offers $5.
- Even though you wanted $10, you suddenly feel like $7 sounds "fair."

That $5 offer became an **anchor**, pulling the whole conversation closer to it.

But if you start by saying $10, now **you** set the anchor – and your friend may adjust their offer higher.

Why it's important

Understanding anchoring helps you:

- Recognize when someone else is setting an anchor
- Stay confident in your own numbers and goals
- Use the first number carefully when making offers
- Avoid being pulled off track by random suggestions

Smart negotiators control the anchor – they don't just accept it.

Try this!

Practice anchoring with a friend or family member:

Pick an item you might trade or sell.

Start the conversation by naming your price first.

Notice how the conversation changes depending on who speaks up first!

13

Reciprocity

Give to get

What it means

Reciprocity is the idea that when you do something nice or helpful for someone, they often feel like doing something nice back.

It's part of how people build trust and fairness in relationships, deals, and everyday life.

Smart negotiators know that **giving first** can lead to better cooperation and outcomes.

Here's an example

You're asking your sibling to help you clean up a big mess.

Instead of just demanding, you start by saying:

- "I'll help you organize your room later if you help me now."
- Or, "I saved you the last cookie from lunch!"

By giving first, you make the other person want to return the favor.

Why it's important

Understanding reciprocity helps you:

- Build stronger friendships and partnerships
- Create win–win situations where both sides benefit
- Avoid one-sided deals where only one person gives
- Make others feel respected and valued

Smart negotiators know that generosity often comes back around.

Try this!

Think of someone you'd like help from this week.

Ask yourself: *What small favor or kindness can I offer first?*

Then see how reciprocity shapes the conversation!

14

Starting With Why

Know your purpose before you decide

What it means

Before you make a choice, a plan, or a deal, it helps to ask: **Why am I doing this?**

This idea comes from leadership expert **Simon Sinek**, who wrote a famous book called *Start With Why*. He studied how great leaders and companies inspire people – and he found they all begin with a clear sense of purpose.

When you understand your **Why** – your purpose or goal – you make smarter decisions and avoid wasting time or energy on things that don't matter.

Here's an example

You want to save money.

You could:

- Save for no reason (just because someone told you to)
- Or save because you have a goal, like buying a bike or going on a special trip

When you know **why** you're saving, you're more motivated, make better tradeoffs, and stick to your plan.

Why it's important

Starting with Why helps you:

- Stay focused on your true goals
- Avoid getting distracted by unimportant details
- Make decisions that align with what matters most to you
- Feel more confident in the choices you make

Smart decision-makers **always** know their Why.

Try this!

Think of a goal you have right now.

Ask yourself:

- Why do I want this?
- What will it help me do or become?

Write down your Why and use it as your guide this week.

15

Prioritization

Put first things first

What it means

Prioritization is the skill of figuring out what's **most important** and making sure you handle it before everything else.

Smart decision-makers don't just make long to-do lists – they decide what needs attention **right now**, what can wait, and what might not matter at all.

Here's an example

You have a busy Saturday:

- Finish your homework
- Help with chores
- Go to a friend's birthday party
- Play video games

If you prioritize, you might decide:

1. Homework first (due tomorrow)
2. Then chores (important to your family)
3. Then the party (if there's time)
4. Video games (after everything else)

Without prioritization, you might waste time on the least important things – and scramble later.

Why it's important

Prioritization helps you:

- Focus on what matters most
- Avoid last-minute stress or mistakes
- Make sure important tasks don't get lost in the mix
- Feel more organized and in control

Smart thinkers **don't** treat everything as equally urgent.

Try this!

Make a list of five things you need to do this week.

Now number them:

- 1 = most important
- 5 = least important

Did anything surprise you about what deserves top priority?

Part 4

Big-Picture Decision-Making

Seeing beyond yourself

"The best way to predict the future is to create it."
— Peter Drucker, management expert

Up to now, we've focused on the choices you make for **yourself** – your time, your money, your effort.

But here's the truth: **your choices affect others, too**.

In this section, you'll learn:

- What *public goods* are, and why they matter
- Why shared resources need careful use *(tragedy of the commons)*
- How groups make fair decisions *(governance)*
- How to plan for surprises *(risk management & Murphy's Law)*
- And why doing the right thing isn't always the easy thing *(ethics)*

Big-picture thinkers understand that good decisions help **everyone**, not just themselves.

Let's zoom out and explore the bigger world of decision-making!

16

Public Goods

Things we all share and enjoy

What it means

Public goods are things that everyone can use and enjoy – whether or not they helped pay for them.

They're often provided by the community or government, like parks, clean air, or streetlights.

No one gets left out, and one person using them doesn't stop others from enjoying them too.

Here's an example

Think about a playground in your neighborhood.

- Everyone can play there, even if they didn't help build it.
- One kid swinging or sliding doesn't stop others from using the rest of the playground.

That's a **public good** – something that's open to all and meant to be shared.

Why it's important

Understanding public goods helps you:

- Appreciate things we all share
- Recognize why it's important to take care of public spaces
- Understand how communities work together to help everyone
- Become a more thoughtful, caring member of your group or neighborhood

Smart thinkers look for ways to protect and enjoy what we all share.

Try this!

Visit a local public space, like a park, library, or schoolyard.

Ask yourself:

- How is this space helping **everyone**?
- What can you do to help take care of it?

17

Tragedy of the Commons

Why shared resources need care

What it means

The **tragedy of the commons** happens when people overuse or waste things that are meant to be shared – because everyone thinks about **what they want** without thinking about the group.

If everyone takes **more than their fair share**, the whole system can break down – and nobody benefits.

Here's an example

Imagine your class has a big jar of markers for everyone to use.

If

- Everyone takes good care of them, they last a long time.

But if

- Even some kids leave the caps off or sneak some home to use, the markers dry out or disappear and soon, nobody can use them.

In the second case, the **shared stuff** is ruined because no one thought about the group.

Why it's important

Understanding the tragedy of the commons helps you:

- Take care of shared things
- Think about how your actions affect others
- Help make fair rules that protect what matters
- Work together so everyone benefits

Smart thinkers look beyond "what's best for me" – they also think about "what's best for everyone."

Try this!

Think of something you share with others – like classroom supplies, family snacks, or park equipment.

How can you help make sure everyone gets a fair share, now and in the future?

18

Governance

How groups make fair decisions

What it means

Governance is the way a group organizes itself to make decisions, set rules, and solve problems fairly.

It's like the "brains" of a team, club, school, or even a country – helping everyone work together and agree on what's best.

Here's an example

You and your friends want to form a soccer team.

You need to decide:

- Who plays which positions
- How to handle disagreements
- What rules everyone will follow

Good governance means you work together, make fair decisions, and follow the rules you set as a group.

Why it's important

Understanding governance helps you:

- Work better in teams or groups
- Respect fair rules and decisions
- Speak up and share your ideas
- Help solve problems instead of causing them

Smart thinkers don't just follow the rules – they help **make** them.

Try this!

Next time you're in a group activity (like a game, club, or project), ask:

- How are decisions being made?
- Are the rules fair and clear?
- What could you do to help improve teamwork?

Risk Management and Murphy's Law

Expect surprises and plan ahead

What it means

Risk management means thinking about what could go wrong and making a plan to handle it.

And here's where **Murphy's Law** comes in:

"Anything that can go wrong, will go wrong."

It's a funny way of saying that surprises and mistakes are part of life – so smart thinkers plan ahead.

FUN FACT!

Murphy's Law is named after an engineer, **Edward A. Murphy Jr.,** who worked on safety tests in the 1940s.

He was known for saying, **"If anything can go wrong, it will"** – and the phrase stuck!

Here's an example

You're planning a picnic. You check the weather, and it's supposed to be sunny, but you bring an umbrella *just in case* it rains.

That's **risk management**: preparing for possible problems.

Murphy's Law reminds you that sometimes, things don't go as planned – even if you try your best.

Why it's important

Understanding risk and Murphy's Law helps you:

- Avoid being caught off guard
- Stay calm when things change or go wrong
- Think ahead and prepare backup plans
- Make better decisions under pressure

Smart thinkers don't expect everything to go perfectly – they plan for the "what if."

Try this!

Think of something you're planning this week – like a trip, event, or project.

- What could go wrong?
- How can you prepare for that?

That's your risk management plan!

20

Ethics

Doing the right thing, even when it's hard

What it means

Ethics is about knowing what's right and fair – and choosing to do the right thing, even when it's difficult.

It's not just about following rules because someone tells you to.

It's about listening to your own sense of honesty, fairness, and kindness.

Here's an example

Imagine you find a wallet on the playground.

You could:

- Keep the money for yourself
- Or turn it in to the office so the owner can get it back

Ethics means **doing the right thing**, even if no one's watching and even if it would be easy to get away with the wrong choice.

Why it's important

Understanding ethics helps you:

- Build trust with others
- Feel proud of your choices
- Be a leader and set a good example
- Make the world a better, fairer place

Smart thinkers know that success isn't just about winning – it's about doing the right thing.

Try this!

Think of a time when you had to make a tough choice between what was easy and what was right.

- What did you decide?
- How did you feel afterward?

That's your ethics at work!

Business Brain Challenge

Can You Plan a Smart Choice?

You've learned so much in this book about how to think like a smart decision-maker – now it's time to put that brainpower to work!

Your challenge: Pick one **real-life decision** you're facing right now.

It could be:

- What to do with your allowance
- How to spend your weekend
- Whether to start a new hobby or project
- Anything else you're trying to figure out!

📝 Step 1: Think of Different Options

- Write down the decision you need to make.
- What are your **options**?

⚖️ Step 2: Spot the Tradeoffs

For each option:

- What are the **opportunity costs**?
- What are the **tradeoffs**?
- What might go wrong, and how could you plan for it?

⭐ Step 3: Prioritize

Which option best fits:

- Your goals?
- Your time and resources?
- Your values? (*Values* are beliefs that are important to you!)

☑ Step 4: Decide!

Make your choice – and write down **why** you picked it.

💭 Step 5: Reflect

After you follow through, ask yourself:

- What worked?
- What would you do differently next time?

🎉 You did it!

Congratulations! You've just completed your **GrowForth Kids Co.** Business Brain Challenge.

Back-Pocket Bonuses

Extra tools and treats for your smart money brain!

You made it to the end – great job!

But just because you've finished reading doesn't mean you're done learning.

We've packed a few extra surprises in this section to help you keep growing your decision-making skills.

Inside, you'll find:

- A **"What I Tried" Log** to track your experiments and adventures
- A **Certificate of Completion** (you earned it!)
- A handy **Glossary** of big words and key ideas from the book
- A **Thank-You Note** from us to you
- And a sneak peek at **other books in the series**!

We hope these back pocket bonuses help you stay curious, keep practicing, and keep growing forth.

"What I Tried" Log

Your very own record of choices and decisions made!

Your brain is like a muscle – the more you exercise it, the stronger it gets! Use this log to track the smart choices you've practiced using the Business Brain Challenge.

Decision #1

My challenge: What real-life decision did I work on?

_____

My options: What choices did I consider?

_____

_____

_____

_____

_____

What I decided: What choice did I make? Why?

_____

_____

What happened: How did it turn out? What went well?

_____

_____

What I learned: What would I do the same next time? What might I change?

_____

_____

Decision #2

My challenge: What real-life decision did I work on?

_____

My options: What choices did I consider?

_____

_____

_____

_____

_____

What I decided: What choice did I make? Why?

_____

_____

What happened: How did it turn out? What went well?

_____

_____

What I learned: What would I do the same next time? What might I change?

_____

_____

Decision #3

My challenge: What real-life decision did I work on?

_____

My options: What choices did I consider?

_____

_____

_____

_____

_____

What I decided: What choice did I make? Why?

_____

_____

What happened: How did it turn out? What went well?

_____

_____

What I learned: What would I do the same next time? What might I change?

_____

_____

Decision #4

My challenge: What real-life decision did I work on?

_____

My options: What choices did I consider?

_____

_____

_____

_____

_____

What I decided: What choice did I make? Why?

_____

_____

What happened: How did it turn out? What went well?

_____

_____

What I learned: What would I do the same next time? What might I change?

_____

_____

Decision #5

My challenge: What real-life decision did I work on?

_____

My options: What choices did I consider?

_____

_____

_____

_____

_____

What I decided: What choice did I make? Why?

_____

_____

What happened: How did it turn out? What went well?

_____

_____

What I learned: What would I do the same next time? What might I change?

_____

_____

GrowForth Kids Co.

Certificate of Completion

Official Proof of Awesomeness

CERTIFICATE OF COMPLETION

Official Proof of Awesomeness

has officially completed:

Book 2: Smart Choices

CERTIFIED DECISION-MAKING BRAIN

They've explored how smart choices shape everyday life, how to weigh costs and benefits, how to plan ahead, negotiate, and think about the big picture. They've learned to spot tradeoffs, manage risks, and make decisions that help themselves and others.

Most of all, they've shown that they're ready to *Grow Forth.*

Glossary
Big Words Made Simple

Anchoring: The first number or idea in a conversation that pulls everything else closer to it.

BATNA: The Best Alternative to a Negotiated Agreement (BATNA) is your backup plan if a deal doesn't work out.

Diminishing Marginal Returns: When adding more effort or resources gives you less extra benefit than before.

Effective Hourly Rate (EHR): How much money you really make per hour after subtracting time, effort, and costs.

Ethics: Knowing what's right and fair – and doing the right thing, even when it's hard.

Governance: How a group organizes itself to make decisions and solve problems fairly.

Marginal Benefit: The extra good or satisfaction you get from doing a little more.

Marginal Cost: The extra time, money, or effort needed to add one more of something.

Murphy's Law: A saying that reminds us anything that can go wrong, might go wrong – so it's smart to plan ahead.

Opportunity Cost: What you give up when you choose one thing over another.

Pareto Principle: Also known as the 80/20 Rule, it's the idea that 80% of results often come from just 20% of the effort or input.

Parkinson's Law: The idea that a task will take as long as the time you give it.

Prioritization: Figuring out what's most important and doing it first.

Public Goods: Things everyone can use and enjoy, like parks, streetlights, and clean air.

Reciprocity: The idea that when you give or help, people often want to give or help back.

Risk Management: Thinking ahead about what could go wrong and making a plan to handle it.

Sunk Cost: Money, time, or effort you've already spent and can't get back.

Tradeoffs: The choices and sacrifices you make when you can't have everything at once.

Tragedy of the Commons: What happens when shared things are overused or wasted because people only think about themselves.

A Thank-You from GrowForth Kids Co.

Hey there, Smart Thinker!

We just want to say **thank you** for reading this book and for using your brainpower to explore how everyday decisions shape your world.

By reading, practicing, and thinking carefully about your choices, you're already growing into someone who can:

- Make smart, thoughtful decisions
- Solve problems with confidence
- Help others and make a positive difference

That's the kind of kid we're proud to know!

This is just the beginning of your journey. Keep asking questions, keep challenging yourself, and keep **growing forth**.

We can't wait to see what you do next!

— Your friends at **GrowForth Kids Co.**

Behind the Book

Meet the Authors

Hi! We're **Matthew** and **Scott MacMillan** – a father-and-son duo from Toronto, Canada who teamed up to write this book together.

Scott (the dad!) is an entrepreneur, former Boston Consulting Group (BCG) strategy consultant, and the author of *Entrepreneur to Author*. He now runs a publishing company that helps experts turn their ideas into books that grow their business (Parents, learn more at: www.grammarfactory.com).

Matthew (the kid!) is full of clever ideas, sharp questions, and curious thinking – especially about money, business, and how the world works. He's also the author of *The Super Poo Official Character Guide*, which launched his own creative publishing journey.

One day, Matthew asked something simple but smart:

"How does a business work?"

That kicked off a ton of conversations – about saving, earning, running a business, and making smart decisions. The more we talked, the more we realized: this stuff isn't just for grown-ups. In fact, kids who learn these ideas early can use them to do some pretty amazing things. So we decided to write the kind of book we both wish existed earlier – clear, fun, and full of real tools for thinking like a **business brain**.

We've got a whole series planned and hope you'll come along for the ride.

Thanks for reading, learning, and growing with us!

— **Matthew & Scott**

Want to keep up with the latest books, tools, and challenges from GrowForth Kids Co.? Visit **www.growforthpress.com** to stay in the loop!

You Might Also Like…

If you liked Book 2, *Smart Choices*, we've got good news – there's more where this came from!

Here's a peek at the other books in the **GrowForth Kids Co. Business Brain Series**:

Book 1 (Available Now!)

How Money Works: Learn How to Earn It, Save It, Grow It, and Spend It Wisely

Learn the basics of money: what it is, how it works and how to use it. Topics: Revenue, expenses, profit, giving, values, and more.

Book 2 (THIS Book)

Smart Choices: The Economics of Everyday Decisions

Learn to make better choices with your time, money, and energy. Topics: Opportunity cost, sunk cost, marginal thinking, tradeoffs, and more.

Book 3 (Coming Soon!)

Let's Start a Business! Your First Steps into Entrepreneurship

Discover how to launch and run a simple business (like a lemonade stand... but smarter!). Topics: Break-even point, marketing, USP, sales, and scaling.

Book 4 (Coming Soon!)

Team Up! How People Work Together to Get Big Things Done

Explore what makes teamwork work – and how different strengths can build something great. Topics: Division of labor, KPIs, public goods, comparative advantage, and more.

Book 5 (Coming Soon!)

Thinking Like a Business Brain: Mindset, Strategy & Making an Impact

Learn how to think like a leader – with purpose, ethics, and long-term thinking. Topics: Strategy vs. tactics, innovation, risk, continuous improvement, and values.

...and that's only the first 5 book! Big things are coming...

Want to know when the next book is out?

Visit **www.growforthpress.com** to explore upcoming titles, get free resources, and join the GrowForth Kids Co. community.